IT'S GOING TO HAPPEN

You Can Birth Your Visions and Dreams

BY

FUNMI JOY ADEOYIN

Some details in stories and anecdotes have been changed to protect identities.

First Editor: Meagan Nicole

Second Editor: Lekan Adeoyin

Cover Design by Mr. Kee Paul

ISBN 978-1-7326234-0-8

Printed in the United States of America

CONTENTS

DEDICATION

I dedicate this book to my Lord and Savior, Jesus Christ. Thank you for taking me as I was but not leaving me as I was.

ACKNOWLEDGMENTS

My Husband - this book is the fruit of your labor.
Thanks for everything. I love you.

My Children - your love for me keeps me going. Thank you for being the best children ever.

My Parents and Parents in Love – you birthed us, raised us and support us. We are eternally grateful.

My Siblings, Siblings in Love and your children – thank you for everything.

My Spiritual Leaders and Mentors – thank you for your love, prayers and encouragement.

My Editors – Thank you hubby and thank you Meagan Nicole. You are both good at what you do.

My Graphic Artist – Thank you Mr. Kee Paul for the cover design. I am so grateful.

My Photographer and Makeup Artist – Tunde and Tobi Adebiyi. You both are truly gifted.

INTRODUCTION

Some years back, I was inspired to give thanks every day for one hundred days. So, daily, I would post on social media about something or someone I was thankful for. I was faithful most days, and on the few days I didn't get to post, I made sure to post twice on the following day. On the last day, I posted about how I had just completed my one hundred days of intentional thanksgiving and how thankful I was to have completed it. Someone commented on my post about how they thought I had been promoting my book for the past one hundred days. That was another nudge to write my book. That person had no idea that I had been seriously considering writing a book that will be a blessing to others.

I have spent my entire adult life stepping out of the uncomfortable and putting together the pieces of my broken soul, and I detail all the lessons I learned along the way in this book. I went from not having the energy or confidence to live my best life to birthing my visions and dreams. I have written this book so that you can follow along on my journey from beginning to present. I share my experiences, my mistakes, my heartaches and my triumphs.

My goal in writing this book is to come alongside you like a midwife does with a woman in labor. In life, we sometimes go through challenges that are painful and overwhelming but with the right help from the right person, we can get guidance and support for life's journey and accomplish something bigger than us, like a pregnant woman who gives birth to her baby with the support of her midwife. This book is for everyone, but you will particularly benefit from reading this book if you feel stuck or hopeless, like you are nobody, or that nobody cares about you. If you have something that you have been looking to accomplish but it seems impossible, I am here to tell you that it's going to happen! With the right information and support, you have everything it takes to birth your vision and dreams.

My prayer is that, after reading this book, any chains holding you bound will be broken and you will be healed from the brokenness in your life. I pray that God's Word and the lessons in this book help you accomplish what you need the most in your life.

Chapter 1

GROWTH IN THE UNCOMFORTABLE

---◉---

People rarely like to step into the uncomfortable. The idea of being in a situation that stretches you and is completely out of the norm can be nerve-racking and scary. I spent most of my childhood and teen years staying away from things and people who made me feel uncomfortable. Trust me—this is no way to live. I was a prisoner in my own mind and wasn't truly living. I used to look at people hanging out, taking on challenges, and living life and wonder how they did that. I intentionally avoided the discomforts of life because I simply didn't want to deal with it and, to be honest, I didn't have the tools to deal with many uncomfortable situations because I avoided them without realizing that I was avoiding growth. I didn't realize that living my life as if in a fetal position all day long was no way to live.

GROW UP

I eventually got to a point where I could no longer live a life without discomforts. I had to come out of my comfort zone, and I had to work on myself and leave the stagnated world that I had created for myself behind. Being a mature adult is no easy feat, and the adult that I have worked so hard to be is the stark opposite of who I used to be. As an adult, I can no longer keep to myself all day because of the fear of being hurt or being made uncomfortable. "Adulting" requires you to go out there and earn a living. It requires you to interact with people regardless of their approach or viewpoints. There are bills to be paid and responsibilities to be taken care of, so being in a bubble isn't going to cut it.

For me, meeting my husband and getting married to him was the beginning of the hard work in my journey to growth and maturity. At the time I met my husband, I barely knew my left hand from my right hand, so to speak, and was an emotional mess. I often cringe when I think back on those years and how difficult I must have been to deal with. My husband was and is a mature man and I learned and continue to learn a lot from him.

If you are in a similar place, please get a mentor! You cannot do it alone. If you knew exactly how to help yourself grow and mature, I am guessing you would have accomplished that already. If you are like me, you would ask God to send you someone who can guide you on the right path, you would read great books from great minds, or you might join a Bible-believing church and become a volunteer! That provides you with accountability and community. I vividly remember the first church that I actively served in and the lessons I learned during that season and how those lessons have carried me through different situations. As those lessons begin to unfold in this book, I pray that you will be blessed by them as well.

GENERATIONAL IMPACT

At some point in my journey, I became a wife and mother, and I knew that if I continued to act without limitations and boundaries, I ran the risk of my children following suit so I needed to get my attitude, actions, and mindset under control. Knowingly or unknowingly, children pick up a lot from their parents and they may lean towards acting like you so, parents, please mold your children with care.

Your transformation from the inside out is bigger than you; it could impact generations, so press in and make the necessary changes. Future generations will either bless your memory or curse you; it's your choice.

SENSITIVE MUCH

During the pruning period of my life, people's words used to hurt me very easily –- whether the person intended to hurt me or not. Also, when I got upset, I could throw a little tantrum whether it was in private or public. This personality flaw was one of the first things that I needed to outgrow, and I did.

As a volunteer leader of those wonderful youths at the church many years ago, I remember an incident that happened early on. Someone said something that I thought was offensive, and everyone was looking to me for leadership and my reaction. Unfortunately, I started throwing a tantrum in front of everyone. It was at that moment that I realized that I needed to outgrow that reaction. The shame I felt in that moment knowing that the people I was responsible for were keeping it together better than I was, freed me from my immaturity. If they could get a grip, I could get a grip.

5

That realization would not have happened if I wasn't in an environment where I was held accountable. It would not have happened in my comfort zone where I would have been isolated in my own world.

I was so used to being a victim that I couldn't see my flaws, but being in an environment of faith and the Word of God, I realized that I wasn't a victim and that I could be better. I have learned to manage my sensitive nature by recognizing that the people who hurt me are themselves likely broken, and many of them did not mean to hurt me.

As a sensitive person, I have found that I can easily sense people's feelings and emotions, but I should be careful not to allow those feelings to overwhelm me. Although what people say or do may cut you deep, you must be quick to pour your heart out to Jesus in prayer and slow to lash out at people. You may think that you need to speak your mind or clap back, but the tactful thing is to choose your words carefully so that things don't get blown out of proportion.

RESOLVE THE ANGER ISSUES

To make matters worse, I had anger issues. I remember being a mess and out of control. Back then, it didn't matter who you were. You could be an elder or a kid but if you made me angry, I had to tell you exactly how I felt in that moment without controlling my words and emotions. A sign of immaturity.

It didn't take much to make me upset, and I never considered the fact that many of the things that were making me upset were things that a mature person would have overlooked. After my rants, I was left worn-out and embarrassed for making a fool of myself. Not a good way to live.

You see, for as far back as I can remember, I have always been bold in speaking out about what I believe in but, sadly, I channeled that energy in the wrong direction. I spent my time boldly telling off people who annoyed me--what a waste of energy and gifts!

I now realize that boldness and passion were placed inside of me to let people know about the love of God, to correct people in love, and to help people birth their visions and dreams. The enemy is more aware of our talents than we are, and he may hijack those talents if we are not careful. Let us all be sure to use every part of our lives to the glory of God.

> *"Be angry, and do not sin': do not let the sun go down on your wrath, nor give place to the devil."* — Ephesians 4:26–27 (NKJV)

When someone or a situation in the church would annoy me, I used to mouth off in the church both directly and indirectly without regard for God or His people because I was upset. The only way I knew of to deal with the situation was to tell somebody off.

I am reminded of a time when a friend was kind enough to refer a client to me. Unfortunately, that client's personality was very difficult for me to manage. I endured for so long, and I think I was losing my mind. Eventually, I decided to reach out to the lovely friend who made the referral. Sadly, it was at a time when I was the angriest about the situation. I left the friend a voice mail in that upset state, ranting about how painful the experience had been and asking her to please speak to the client about her conduct. I still cringe when I think about that incident. I wish I had left that message after I had cooled off. I would have chosen softer words and wouldn't have blamed the person who tried to help my business. Anger can do that, so be wise.

The thing about anger is this: many times, we let our anger get the better part of us. When we are angry, we should try our best not to say anything or do anything, especially something that we might regret. If we don't exercise self-control when angry, it may lead to embarrassment and humiliation. You might say or do something that you might regret. So, take some time to cool off!

When angry about a situation, address the problem when the anger has subsided and not in the heat of the moment. If this is hard for you as it was for me, seek help from the Lord. Calmly addressing issues is not a sign of weakness but rather a sign of strength and self- control. Remember that the key is to refrain from saying something that you will regret.

There are times when you need to approach your offender but that requires much prayer, wisdom, and having no unrealistic expectations because the person may not be willing to have a peaceful conversation. You should accept that and move on with a pure heart but keep the person in your prayers because God can change hearts.

"The king's heart is in the hand of the LORD, Like the rivers of water; He turns it wherever He wishes." — Proverbs 21:1 (NKJV)

LET IT GO

The act of praying for a person who hurt you is something that the devil never saw coming. The expectation of the enemy is for you to live in bitterness and hate or to clap back, but you and I must rise above the pain in love. I choose to pray for the people who have wronged me, and I spend my time asking God to heal them and fix whatever is broken in them as I pray the same for myself. This helps to heal the hurt and accomplish my goal of being at peace with everyone. Remember that prayer is not a one-time deal. You keep praying until that person's hurt is healed. The Word of God is clear:

> *"But I say to you, love your enemies, bless those who curse you, do good to those who hate you, and pray for those who spitefully use you and persecute you, that you may be sons of your Father in heaven; for He makes His sun rise on the evil and on the good, and sends rain on the just and on the unjust." — Matthew 5:44–45 (NKJV)*
>
> *"Pursue peace with all people, and holiness, without which no one will see the Lord." — Hebrews 12:14 (NKJV)*

Don't let the pain of what someone has done to you cloud your judgment. As hard as it is to let the pain go, it is worse for you to hold on to the pain. Unforgiveness is like a blessing blocker. It stands as a hindrance between you and what God wants to do in your life. Plus, forgiveness is for you; it's not for them. Don't let anyone use you as a dumpster. Get that garbage out of your system and live free. Praying for them works to accomplish this.

FOCUS ON YOU

During a season in my life, I began meeting a lot of new people whose personalities and thinking patterns were very different from mine. This is to be expected in life, but it was difficult for a person who had spent many years avoiding necessary interactions. The truth is that we all have different personalities. Not everyone will talk, think, react, or even treat you in the way that you would prefer. Growth has taught me that I cannot control anyone but me. When I made this realization, I pressed into working on myself; I took responsibility for my life and my actions, and I stopped worrying about what anyone thought of me.

I have learned to accommodate the weaknesses in other people's personalities rather than trying to fix them. Sometimes, we fall into the trap of focusing on someone else's personality flaw rather than ours, but everyone has an area of weakness in their own life that needs work. It is more productive to spend time working on our own flaws than someone else's. Like the Bible says,

> *"You hypocrite, first take the plank out of your own eye, and then you will see clearly to remove the speck from your brother's eye" (Matthew 7:5, NIV).*

If you focus on fixing others rather than yourself, you will end up offending people, burning bridges, and creating enemies. Focusing on others' flaws could lead to hatred for people, which is counterproductive. But if you focus on your flaws and fix them, people will observe your growth and be positively impacted. It is a more challenging but more productive route.

"We do this by keeping our eyes on Jesus, the champion who initiates and perfects our faith. Because of the joy awaiting him, he endured the cross, disregarding its shame. Now he is seated in the place of honor beside God's throne." — Hebrews 12:2 (NLT)

We need the wisdom of God to know which battles to pick and which ones to let go. You must resist the temptation to fight every battle otherwise you will be bruised, battered, and worn out, and you may find yourself under-achieving in key areas of your life.

Each day, God gives us the energy and strength that we need for accomplishing and achieving destiny. Don't give that energy to quarrels, round the clock TV and social media, and other time wasters. You don't want to look up and realize that you have left undone many things that you could have done to bless your generation because your energy was used up fighting unnecessary battles.

TAKE CORRECTION

Another area of growth for me has been learning obedience and taking correction. I grew up in a situation where I raised myself and did whatever I wanted and acted however I liked. But a self-centered way of living doesn't work in marriage, as a mother, or as a child of God.

It was much easier to lean on my own understanding and do things my way. However, that road was not leading me to growth but was keeping me stagnant. I had to learn to respect the input and voices of authority over my life and give them their due honor. I had to learn to place my trust in God and His plan for my life. God's Word is to be honored in my life and so should my husband, my parents, and other God-ordained voices of influence in my life.

We need to understand that God strategically places people around us, and He speaks to us through them from time to time. If you are one to shut down every input, you will sometimes block out good advice from godly sources. No one person knows it all. Do not discount the advice of godly counsel because God could be speaking to you through them. Discernment is key!

I remember that my sweet mentor at the time would always pull me aside in love, and she would encourage me not to let anger get the better part of me. With time, prayer, and the proper application of the Word, I learned how to process my feelings properly and that I must not speak harshly to people.

My husband has also been that Godly voice that corrects me and guides me. He is such an amazing covering and a gift from God. Ask God to lead you to someone who can hold you accountable and correct you in love and, when they do, please follow their guidance. It can be life-giving and life-changing.

THE MIND OF CHRIST

Having the right mindset is very critical to a person's growth. Just because you feel a certain way doesn't mean that the feeling is accurate. You may feel like kicking a person—and that feeling may be valid—but that doesn't mean that the feeling is going to lead you to make a right decision. So, we should be careful about basing our entire existence on our feelings.

Also, we need to work on processing information the right way. You can either look at a situation and create the worst-case scenario in your mind or give the benefit of the doubt and show more understanding toward others. Reaching for the worst-case scenario and believing the worst about people does not help solve differences. I recognize that this is easier said than done and a person that is broken on the inside processes information through the lens of their pain. It is my honor to let you know that whatever pain you are going through, Jesus can heal! Put your trust in Him and cry out to Him for help with all sincerity. He will help you, and your life will never be the same again.

> *"For, 'Who can know the LORD's thoughts? Who knows enough to teach him?' But we understand these things, for we have the mind of Christ." — 1 Corinthians 2:16 (NLT)*

I pray 1 Corinthians 2:16 over my mind regularly, asking that God should give me the mind of Christ. You can too!

Chapter 2

KNOW YOURSELF

---

*E*ach of us is a spirit; we have a soul, and we live in a body. It may sound like a cliché, but it is part of the knowledge that we must have about ourselves. Each of us ought to know what our likes, dislikes, strengths, weakness, etc., are.

I was a pre-teen in boarding school when one of my dorm mates and I were having a dispute, which was typical of me back then. For some reason, I was silly enough to point out how big I thought her nose was. She burst out laughing and got the attention of a few people close by. They were then asked to judge who had the bigger nose between the two of us. The verdict was unanimous: I had the bigger nose. I learned a big lesson that day; I had zero self-awareness, and I needed to spend more time knowing myself and less time picking on others.

We need to learn to know ourselves from an objective perspective. If someone were to ask you if you were a nice person, you might answer "yes" but in reality, people might perceive you as someone that isn't nice. You can become more self-aware. You can ask questions of inquiry from people who have your best interest at heart. Ask them to describe you in an honest and sincere way. Also, be ready for whatever feedback you get. Don't let the information crush you but use it as a stepping stone for self-development.

YOUR BODY; YOUR SCARS; IMPERFECTLY PERFECT

As a mother who has birth three children, my body is not what it used to be, but I love my imperfect body. I am aware of every beauty that my body exudes. I am also aware of the parts of my body that would be considered imperfect. It has taken many years of hard work, but I love me. The vain things of this world do not define me. I will get on Facebook and Instagram live without makeup in a heartbeat because I am comfortable in my own skin, and I truly love me. Also, makeup is a beauty enhancer, not my crutch. I write all these to encourage you to love yourself. If you are a mother, and the birth of your child or children has changed your body, it is not the end of the world. You can love who you are, how you are while working on getting yourself to where you need to be. You are beautiful with or without makeup. You are beautiful with or without scars. It doesn't matter if your self-hate is as deep as mine was, you can put in the work and learn to speak about yourself in positive terms.

I am reminded of the scar on my right ankle that I got as a teenager in boarding school. I remember striking my leg against a big rock while running. It hurt badly. I remember that I would not be caught wearing a skirt without also wearing my ankle bracelet.

As I write this, it occurs to me that the ankle bracelet was more like the ankle monitor that criminal offenders wear. The monitor shows that they have committed a crime, that their movement is restricted, and that the authorities can track them. In my case, I felt bad about myself, and I told myself that I could hide behind an ankle bracelet. I restricted myself to skirts and an ankle bracelet, and I allowed the enemy to restrict me by believing his lies. I am grateful for the freedom that I found in my Lord and Savior, Jesus Christ! I am reminded of a song called "No Longer Slaves" written by Jonathan David Helser, Brian Joel Case, and Mark Johnson that says, "I'm no longer a slave to fear; I am a child of God. And I say: I'm no longer a slave to sin, I am a child of God."

You may have acne on your face, or an imperfection on your body that may be a cause of concern for you, I would like to remind you that you are God's masterpiece. Love you and wear your scars like a battle scar. It is proof that you have lived and that you are still here! Your scar tells a story that makes you unique. You have the power to stop hiding behind your scar but rather let your light so shine that no scar can stand in your way.

THE BROKENNESS

I would describe my childhood experience as that of a broken child. Growing up, I felt rejected, unstable, and unloved. Not enough attention was given to me. I felt that my needs weren't met and that I was being silenced. It seemed like my opinions didn't carry much weight. This is not to say that nobody loved or cared for me, but those were my feelings. I carried that spirit of rejection with me for many years. It has taken years of self-examination to be able to articulate this part of me and work through it.

I had to learn that the reason I was always "fighting" people was because I felt that it was me against the world and that everyone was trying to silence me, and I was not going to let that happen. I was trying to gain a sense of power that I felt I had lost.

Children who are being bullied sometimes act out, especially if they feel like nobody cares and no one is listening. It is important for parents to consider the root cause of their child's behavior for the sake of the child's well-being. Parents should pay attention to the dynamics in their home, and make sure that none of your children lack the attention they need.

BROKEN MIND?

I am reminded of a season of my life, when I felt like my mind was broken. I was bombarded with and tormented by horrible thoughts round-the-clock for several months. It was troubling but with the Lord and His word on my side, I got through it. You may also feel like your mind is broken. Perhaps your mind seems to be flooded with thoughts that you didn't choose. The thoughts may be nasty, unwanted, or troubling. Rest assured because I would like to introduce you to your new best friend – the Word of God which says:

> *"We demolish arguments and every pretension that sets itself up against the knowledge of God, and we take captive every thought to make it obedient to Christ." — 2 Corinthians 10:5 (NIV)*

As soon as each thought comes into your mind, say, "I capture you and command you to be obedient to Christ in the name of Jesus!" Do this each time, and don't stop doing it until the thoughts are under control.

If the bad thoughts continue in your sleep in the form of nightmares, keep declaring the word of the Lord! Speak these Scriptures to those thoughts and nightmares:

> *"From now on, let no one cause me trouble, for I bear on my body the marks of Jesus."* — *Galatians 6:17 (NIV)*
>
> *"You, dear children, are from God and have overcome them, because the one who is in you is greater than the one who is in the world."* — *1 John 4:4 (NIV)*

THE REJECTION

I remember carrying with me a strong sense of rejection. Back then, I was described as "clingy." Whenever I had an opportunity to sleep over at someone's house and was treated nicely as a guest, I would cling to that person and would want to stay past the expected time of departure. Somehow, in my mind, a friendly house host meant comfort and companionship, and I had a hard time detaching from that. I wish I had sought God's warmth rather than the wavering warmth of mere mortals. I wish I understood then that I was being preserved and separated for such a time as this.

It seemed, back then, like everyone around me had friends except me. I wish I had learned how to be content in the one or two friends that I had rather than comparing my life to someone else's. If only I had known myself well enough to consider the fact that I am more of an introvert. If I ever had many friends, I most likely would have been exhausted and worn out trying to keep up with them.

Don't compare your life to someone else's life. You are a masterpiece handcrafted by God Almighty! Perhaps, the life that you covet is a life that you would not be able to manage, so be thankful for what you have.

Overcoming the spirit of rejection took a lot of work. Feeling like nobody values you leaves a big hole in a person's heart. As a mother, I make sure that my kids know that I love them every day, although I will be quick to tell you that I am not perfect.

I am so glad that "God decided in advance to adopt us into his own family by bringing us to himself through Jesus Christ" (Ephesians 1:5a, NLT)

Therefore, you and I no longer have to feel like nobody cares because God does. He has His arms opened wide, waiting for you to come in and be secured in the family of faith where you won't be maltreated but loved with an everlasting love that floods your entire life.

THE EMPTINESS

I also vividly remember feeling empty as a child. In my life, the feeling of emptiness manifested itself as a heavy weight and a seemingly unshakeable sadness. Emptiness keeps your head bowed and robs you of the twinkle that ought to be in your eyes. It strips you of self-confidence and leaves you enduring life rather than enjoying and living life to the fullest.

There are so many void-fillers in this world. There are many different "drugs" of choice to fill the void in a person's life such as, food, alcohol, sex, drugs, TV shows, keeping bad company, etc. But you can't fill the God-shaped hole in your heart with any of these things. You can only fill the God-shaped hole in your heart with God. You can cry out to God with sincerity and ask Him to fill you up and come into your heart. It may sound too silly or too simple, but it's real. It is the gift that has the power to make you whole and change your life. It certainly changed mine.

> *"I pray that out of his glorious riches he may strengthen you with power through his Spirit in your inner being, so that Christ may dwell in your hearts through faith. And I pray that you, being rooted and established in love, may have power, together with all the Lord's holy people, to grasp how wide and long and high and deep is the love of Christ..."*
> — *Ephesians 3:16–18 (NIV)*

LOW SELF-ESTEEM

When a person's confidence is low and they don't feel like they are worth much, they make choices that reflect what little value they place on themselves. Anytime I see a young person off to college who spends time partying and failing out of classes, I wonder what the underlying issue is. Whenever I see a person jumping from sex partner to sex partner, though some people interpret that behavior as confidence and independence, I wonder what the underlying issue is. Whenever I see a person with a promising future surrounded by friends who are going the opposite direction and is influenced by them, I wonder what the underlying issue is.

Low self-esteem or low confidence stems from believing false information about yourself. The Bible says this of the devil's character:

> *"You belong to your father, the devil, and you want to carry out your father's desires. He was a murderer from the beginning, not holding to*

the truth, for there is no truth in him. When he lies, he speaks his native language, for he is a liar and the father of lies." — John 8:44 (NIV)

The devil feeds us so many lies, and the sad part is that we often believe him. To neutralize the devil's lies, you and I must get in the Word of God and stay in the Word daily. We must meditate on what God says in Jeremiah 29:11 (NIV): He truly has "plans to prosper you and not to harm you, plans to give you hope and a future." These words are life to anyone who feels hopeless, and they serve as an anchor for someone who struggles to find direction in life.

Chapter 3

CHOOSE YOUR FRIENDS WISELY

---◉---

*B*ad company corrupts good manners. Bad friends can lead you down a path that you never thought you would travel. Bad friends coupled with low self-esteem is a recipe for disaster. As a child, the elders in my community always said, "Show me your friends, and I'll tell you who you are." Make no mistake: you are your friends, and your friends are you. It will only be a matter of time before you adopt the mindset of your friends, so be wise in your friend choices. These "friends" include people you follow on social media. When you follow or befriend someone, they are leading you somewhere. So, the question is this: where are you going, and are your friends helping you get there, or are they leading you in the opposite direction?

Several years ago, during what I call my "foolish years," I had several friends who were bad for me in every sense, but I could not part with them because I was lonely and longed to be part of a group. Due to my low self-esteem and lack of direction, I followed wherever they led. When they said it was time to party, it was time to party. When they said it was time to get a boyfriend, it was time to get a boyfriend. When they said it was time to lie, it was time to lie. I dressed like them, talked liked them, lived like them, and acted like them. I *was* them. I became very different from who I was prior to meeting them.

WATCH OUT FOR DANGER

Friends can have a lot of influence over a person's life and can put your life in danger, so choose your friends wisely. Don't be like me as a nineteen-year-old. Do not wait for people to select and elect you to be their friend. Consider who you want to become and select people who can come along with you on that journey. It might be just one person that has what it takes to go on that journey with you, and that's OK because bad friends can put your life in danger.

I have a vivid memory of my then-friends asking me to come along on an out-of-state reunion event. Without hesitation, I got in the car with them for a ten-hour car ride to another state. When we got there, we lodged in our hotel, freshened up, and headed over to our evening event. It was a typical party scene, and people were meeting and mingling until late hours of the night.

After the event, my friends wanted to attend an after party, but I wanted to head back to the hotel to get some rest. So, two girls and I got into the back of the vehicle of two male partygoers. I was under the impression that they would drop me off at the hotel and head off to their after-party.

I noticed that we were heading away from the hotel, and I objected and asked them to take me to the hotel. One of my "friends" got angry and asked them to drop me off right then and there, and they did. They kicked me out on the street in the middle of the night dressed in "party clothes." I didn't even have any money on me, and I remember walking back to the hotel hoping that I would not be kidnapped or raped, walking by a bunch of homeless people on the street. God must have been watching over me on the streets because I made it back to the hotel, and I continued to follow those people as friends despite where that friendship had led me. My low self-esteem and rejection issues only worsened in my relationship with those friends.

Eventually, I was ousted from that group because I was in constant dispute with one of the members, and I would not stop telling her off for one reason or the other. I also moved to another state, which marked the end of that relationship unlike in the past when I took breaks from friendships only to return to the dysfunctional setting after some time.

BREAK THE CYCLE

I obviously didn't learn anything from that experience because sometime later, I found a new friend and I still had the same issues. I was invited by that friend to visit them in another state and take a road trip to a neighboring state for yet another reunion. I flew to my friend's house, and by the following day, we were taking our six-hour drive to the neighboring state for the reunion.

There was constant friction again because that was what I was used to and created. I just remember always feeling like people weren't listening to me, so I would stir up all sorts of drama so I would be heard. At the height of the drama, we went out to lunch at a buffet, and I took mine to go.

At dinner time and after our meet and greet, my friend invited a few people who we met to a local restaurant. I was still in my foolish years, and the only money I had was the money for the flight and maybe $20, all of which I had exhausted. So, I sat in the restaurant and didn't order anything because I didn't have any money left! The part that stung the most was that right after everyone had eaten and while I was dying of hunger, my "friend" paid for everyone's meal. It was like a hot knife went through my back, and the only person I could blame was me.

A couple of hours later, we were back at the hotel, and I rushed to the fridge to get the leftovers from lunch and ate it while everyone else went to bed after eating fresh food from a restaurant. A heads-up that the food would be paid for would have been nice!

The truth is that I never should have gone on that trip. And if I were going on that kind of trip, I should have gone with people who truly loved me and those I truly loved. If I were to go on a trip like that, I should be mature enough to handle whatever may come up and to deal with the different personalities of the people on the trip.

GODLY FRIENDSHIPS

The good news is that God can give you a godly friend. Keep in mind that "every good and perfect gift is from above, coming down from the Father of the heavenly lights, who does not change like shifting shadows," (James 1:17, NIV). If you ask God with sincerity of heart, He will give you a friend whose love for you and relationship with you will blow your mind. God is so faithful. He won't let you down because He gets you and knows what you need.

When you finally find that good friend, make sure that you are faithful and honest. You should treasure your good friends and not take them for granted. Good friends are rare, and you ought to treat them as the rarity that they are and honor the relationship.

Godly friendships don't tear you down; they build you up. Godly friends are going in the same direction as you and have the same core values and interests as you. Godly friends love you, have your best interests at heart, and are mutually invested in the relationship. Godly friends won't speak evil about you behind your back; if they have anything to say about you, they will tell you to your face in love. They are people who will pray for you, root for your success, be happy when you are happy, and help you get back up when you fall.

Again, be wise when choosing your friends. Don't allow your loneliness or need to belong to be your guide because those factors can cause you to make bad choices. Don't be unequally yoked in your friendships.

SEASONAL FRIENDSHIPS

Something else that is noteworthy about friendships is that some come in seasons. Don't try to make your seasonal friends permanent! The friend that you had in high school may not necessarily be your friend in college if the relationship has run its course and served its purpose.

Also, some friends are situational. You may have a gym buddy or a prayer buddy or even a cooking buddy. That may be the entire nature of your friendship, and that's OK! Don't make friendships more than what they are. If you are texting your friend every day and that friend only texts or calls you once a year, you might want to scale back and make some assessments.

Also, some friends are low maintenance friends, which means that you may not see or speak to each other often, but you still have the love and bond. Don't overburden those friendships.

Chapter 4

THE LOVE OF GOD

──────────────── ◉ ────────────────

The love that God has for mankind is truly indescribable. I want you to meditate on the Scripture below:

"The LORD your God is with you, the Mighty Warrior who saves. He will take great delight in you; in his love he will no longer rebuke you, but will rejoice over you with singing." — Zephaniah 3:17 (NIV)

HIS LOVE HEALS

The description of the love of God in Zephaniah 3:17 has brought great healing to my soul, and I believe it will help you as well.

I am reminded of a time when my family visited some people who I believed would love me but didn't – at least not in a way that I needed. I was still very much broken at the time. I was also seeking for people to love me deeply but, at the time, I didn't realize that was a huge mistake. People can't give what they don't have. How can you expect someone who is dealing with his or her own brokenness and doesn't have love to give you love? Also, how can you expect someone to love you in a way that only God can?

I remember leaving their house after much hurt and arriving at our next destination. I headed for the bedroom, lay down in a fetal position, and cried and cried. I was under the covers, so no one knew because I cried as quietly as I could.

I poured my heart out to the Lord. I then went online and searched Scriptures on God's love and found Zephaniah 3:17. I just felt in that moment that I needed a steadfast and special love.

I was so comforted by the fact that this Mighty Warrior of a God is also my Savior who delights in me. When you feel like an outcast and unwanted, remember God Almighty delights in you! He always has and He always will. Can you just picture Him rejoicing over you with singing and not rebuking you?

When you are in your growth phase and are being shown your faults for correction purposes, it feels like you are being rebuked. I want you to stay the course; hang in there! Keep your eyes fixed on your end goal and how polished and refined you will be at the end! Keep your mind focused on the image of God rejoicing over you with singing. Just like a mother cradles her precious baby and sings over her child to calm him or her, God does the same with you! Remember that the Lord your God is always with you through all of life's twists and turns.

HIS LOVE SAVES

"But because of his great love for us, God, who is rich in mercy, made us alive with Christ even when we were dead in transgressions—it is by grace you have been saved." — Ephesians 2:4–5 (NIV)

"And hope does not put us to shame, because God's love has been poured out into our hearts through the Holy Spirit, who has been given to us." — Romans 5:5 (NIV)

I am overwhelmed by Ephesians 2:4–5 and Romans 5:5 because they accurately describe how I came to Christ. I remember being lifeless and purposeless and going through the motions of life. My mother came to live with me and started attending a great Bible-believing church. I would occasionally accompany her, but I couldn't care less about the church or anything it stands for.

At some point, we received an invitation to attend a women's breakfast fellowship. My mom planned on attending, but I didn't. She encouraged me to attend as well, but I wasn't interested.

Thankfully, a relative happened to be in town and came visiting. Both the relative and my mother insisted that I attend, so I grudgingly accepted the invitation. We got there on a cold winter morning in February. The fellowship started and we were being taught the Word of God when, suddenly, the woman sitting next to me and I burst out in tears for no apparent reason.

At the time, I had no idea that the book of Ephesians 2:4–5 was in effect in my life. I didn't realize that a great God, rich in mercy, was making this dead soul alive with Christ. In that moment, I was being saved by grace! In that moment, God was pouring His love into my heart through the Holy Spirit, and I felt every drop of His love. I didn't deserve it, but He did it anyway. What amazing grace!

> *"But when the goodness and loving kindness of God our Savior appeared, he saved us, not because of works done by us in righteousness, but according to his own mercy, by the washing of regeneration and renewal of the Holy Spirit..." — Titus 3:4–5 (ESV)*

I want you, amazing reader, to know that on the day you truly surrender your heart to the Lord, the goodness and kindness of the Lord makes a distinct appearance in your life. It is something that a person can't earn by works. It is God's mercy at work to wash our sins away and produce regeneration of life. How I love you, Lord!

UNFAILING LOVE

> *"Long ago, the LORD said to Israel: 'I have loved you, my people, with an everlasting love. With unfailing love I have drawn you to myself.'"* — *Jeremiah 31:3 (NLT)*
>
> *"Know therefore that the LORD your God is God, the faithful God who keeps covenant and steadfast love with those who love him and keep his commandments, to a thousand generations..."* — *Deuteronomy 7:9 (ESV)*
>
> *"For as high as the heavens are above the earth, so great is his steadfast love toward those who fear him." — Psalm 103:11 (ESV)*

> *"May you experience the love of Christ, though it is too great to understand fully. Then you will be made complete with all the fullness of life and power that comes from God." — Ephesians 3:19 (NLT)*

My prayer is that you may also experience the love of Christ as I have. Christ's love is indescribable and life-changing.

Like icing on the cake, God might also place people in your life who will love you in a way that brings you healing. God poured His love into my husband and, ever since I met my husband, his continuous love for me has healed those feelings of rejection. Now that I am a mother, the love of my kids has done the same.

I believe that the love of God can heal rejection. He can also surround you with people who will love you back to life. He is waiting for you with arms wide open, ready to love you like only a good father can.

His love has flooded my heart and made me whole. The love of God fills every void in my heart and my life, and I am overwhelmed looking back to my starting point and seeing how far God has brought me. God's love is so complete.

I don't know who doesn't love you, but I know that God loves you. I don't know who has rejected you, but God wants you. I don't know who makes you feel like nothing, but you ought to know that you are the apple of God's eyes. You mean everything to Him. He loves you perfectly. His love is enough for you.

Chapter 5

LOVE NEVER FAILS

———————————◉———————————

When you have the privilege of experiencing the love of God, you know that it is not something that you can keep to yourself. The love of God should flow freely from Him to us then through us to reach people who need it. Love is not just a feeling; love is a set of principles that we embody. The love of God runs deeply and can heal a broken soul.

THE HURT

Many times, people who hurt us are themselves hurt and broken, hence the phrase, "Hurting people hurt people." I know it can be very difficult to think kindly about the person hurting your feelings and breaking your heart, but it helps to provide a different perspective.

You may find yourself in a situation where you feel like you are surrounded by people who don't understand or value you, and you are angry and bitter about it. You have done everything within your power to get away from them, but you are forced to see them regularly, and even when they are not there, you replay all the offenses in your mind. You were the kind of person that always prided yourself as someone who could never be hateful, but before you knew it, you were drowning in hate toward the person or people who appear to be working together to make your life miserable.

Sure, you have tried to tackle the situation with "an eye for an eye" approach. When they attacked you, the hurt sat in your heart, and you unleashed it on them the next time you had the chance. Not because you were intending to attack, but when hurt and hate lead the way, there are many offences. I just want you to know that love is the only way out of hate.

Ask yourself this question: why do I get so hurt by people in the first place?

I once heard an illustration about a deep wound. Two people of the same strength are walking along. The first has a deep wound on one foot and no wound on the other foot. The second person steps on the wounded foot and the non-wounded foot of the first person with equal force. The result is that the foot with the deep wound is likely to be in more pain than the foot without a wound. The truth is that many people live with deep wounds in their soul from past hurt, abuse, abandonment, rejection, and/or pain and life's situations or people stepping on our toes can result in more pain for them that it would, if no wounds existed.

PRAYER FOR HEALING

It is my greatest honor to introduce you to Jehovah Rapha-the One who can heal you; He sure healed me. I perceive God is asking these questions right now:

"Since my people are crushed, I am crushed; I mourn, and horror grips me. Is there no balm in Gilead? Is there no physician there? Why then is there no healing for the wound of my people?" — Jeremiah 8:21–22 *(NIV)*

You should know that He feels your every pain and hears your cry. He is the greatest Physician to ever exist, and there is no pain or diagnosis that is beyond Him. In Him, your healing is guaranteed and complete. Will you cry out to Him now with sincerity and ask Him to heal you from the inside out? He will make your life so beautiful that you will no longer recognize yourself.

"The Spirit of the Sovereign LORD is on me, because the LORD has anointed me to proclaim good news to the poor. He has sent me to bind up the brokenhearted, to proclaim freedom for the captives and release from darkness for the prisoners, to proclaim the year of the LORD's favor and the day of vengeance of our God, to comfort all who mourn,

and provide for those who grieve in Zion—to bestow on them a crown of beauty instead of ashes, the oil of joy instead of mourning, and a garment of praise instead of a spirit of despair. They will be called oaks of righteousness, a planting of the LORD for the display of his splendor.

"They will rebuild the ancient ruins and restore the places long devastated; they will renew the ruined cities that have been devastated for generations." — Isaiah 61:1–4 *(NIV)*

Through the inspiration of the Holy Spirit, the prophet Isaiah wrote these words and I believe this is what God is saying to you in this season. God has sent me the anointed words in this book to bind up your broken heart. I don't know what happened to you that caused your heart to be broken, but you can receive your healing in the mighty name of Jesus!

I decree that you are free from anything that holds you bound be it food, sex, lust, sin, drugs, alcohol, opioids, low self-esteem, hate, or hurt in the name of Jesus!

I pray that the crown of thorns and ashes upon your head will be replaced with a crown of beauty. You have longed for joy for so long, and your mourning seems to have no end. But I decree by the power that raised Jesus from the dead that the oil of joy begins to flow from your life this season in the name of Jesus!

If you ever feel despair starting to set in, give God praise and thanks! Grab your journal or notepad and begin to write down the things that God has done for you, and be thankful for them. Look at your life from the strengths perspective and live a life of gratitude, knowing that all things will work together for your good.

YOU CAN BIRTH YOUR VISIONS AND DREAMS

I believe I received the strength to live above hate through the birth of my children. I have a type of personality that is very uncomfortable with pain. Because of that, I prayed that God would help me have a supernatural childbirth. A supernatural childbirth occurs when a woman gives birth with little to no pain with the help of the Holy Spirit.

My three pregnancies were anything but easy for me, but by grace, I didn't have any complications. But being pregnant with them weighed heavily on my body. I am only 5' 3," and I gained about thirty pounds during each pregnancy. The third pregnancy was the most intense. The heartburn was epic, and I was only able to drink apple juice. Who knew that orange juice is acidic? Each time I tried drinking orange juice, it burned. I had excess saliva in my mouth throughout the pregnancy, and the smell of cooking food was unbearable.

For my first two deliveries, I had the opportunity to get an epidural, and I gladly obliged because it reduces labor pains. But for my third (and last) baby, I had to have a natural birth. The pain is nothing that I can put into words. The "ring of fire" is supposed to reference earthquake zones, but the ring of fire I know is the pain I felt when that child's head was making its way out. After giving birth, I couldn't even stay awake. I was so exhausted that I slept immediately and for hours. And for all three births, my hip came out of its socket and walking was difficult for a few weeks postpartum.

I write all these to say that though there was a lot of pain, there was also a lot of strength produced during my natural childbirth process.

The pain you are going through is being used to do a work in you that will strengthen you for the journey ahead. None of your experiences are wasted. No pain you have ever felt is for nothing.

"And we know that in all things God works for the good of those who love him, who have been called according to his purpose." — Romans 8:28 (NIV)

So, through pain, I received the strength to overcome hate with love. I made the choice that no matter how terrible I felt about being verbally attacked by the people who hurt me, I would no longer respond out of pain.

> *"No, in all these things we are more than conquerors through him who loved us."* — *Romans 8:37 (NIV)*

As this Scripture expresses, I realized that I was no longer a victim that nobody loved, wanted, picked on, or a person that couldn't express herself. I am now a completely different person. I am loved, blessed; I have been made whole, and I am more than a conqueror.

Afterwards, I could sit through negativity and respond in love until love and joy permeated the atmosphere. All the pain I had gone through had finally produced the strength I needed to overcome the hurt and hate. God's mercy came through, and I am forever changed. I am now well on my way to birthing my visions and dreams!

Chapter 6

PUSH

Figuring out what your purpose is can be a daunting task. We are programmed to go to school, get a job, and keep working until we retire at 65. That is a good plan, but it doesn't work out that way for everyone. I got to a point in my life where I knew deep in my heart that the typical 9 to 5 would pay the bills but would not bring fulfillment. I think you should hold on to your 9 to 5 and keep those bills paid but work on your passion on the side.

HOPE DEFERRED MAKES THE HEART SICK

I had been pushing for quite some time, trying to break through in my finances/career. I went to a four-year college and graduated with a Bachelor's Degree in Business Management. After graduation, I applied everywhere and even went for a few job interviews, but my efforts were unsuccessful. I reassured myself that after I was done with law school, things would turn around for me. So, the fall following college graduation,

I started law school. Three years later, I graduated from law school and sent out my résumé to many law firms but, again, the interviews that I had yielded no good results.

I consoled myself with the fact that though things weren't working out in my career, I had my marriage, kids and church commitments to keep me busy. I got busy with all those responsibilities, but deep down I knew I still wanted to have a career of my own.

After a while, hope turned into despair. I convinced myself that maybe it was my accent or my skin color or my difficult-to-pronounce name, etc. As each year went by, my student loans piled up, my hope dwindled, and I worked unstable jobs here and there. I also tried to work with multilevel marketing companies; from the ones that offer online grocery shopping to the ones that sell body shapers but none of them worked for me. I tried different business ideas as I tried to figure out what I was supposed to be doing.

GUARD AGAINST BAD CHOICES

My quest to make money led me to try selling hair extensions. I saw someone on social media selling it, and I decided to try as well. I really thought that was my big break. So, I set up my website, ordered the hair extensions wholesale, and started posting and asking people for their business.

The problem was that I was in it only to make money. I had no passion for hair and, quite frankly, I don't even like dealing with hair. It was bad. I had no passion for working with hair. I even used the same marketing ideas as the person whose posts about hair extensions I originally saw plus pictures off the internet rather than using original pictures. It was a recipe for disaster.

When someone sent a message to me pointing out everything that was wrong with the business, I shut the whole thing down. It was a burden, not a blessing. I was off and I knew it.

A business, birth out of hunger to make money, that you are not passionate about may end up being a burden and not a blessing. A business that isn't well-researched and is birth out of copying someone else may end up being a burden and not a blessing.

When a woman births a baby, the baby comes from inside the woman not from outside. Therefore, whatever idea or business or whatever it is that you birth, it should come from inside of you, not something external that you felt pressured to do or something you did because someone else seemed to look good doing it.

HIT THE RESET BOTTON

After much toiling, I retraced my steps back to my foundation and Maker: God Almighty. I had to ask Him to give me whatever information that I clearly didn't have about my life. I needed His help to fill in the gaps of my life. I cried to Him, asking Him for help, and He came through.

He had me go back to a local community college for a certificate program, and I also joined a weekend training program for women at the school. I met someone through that training program that walked me through the process of running a law office and here I am today, running my own law office, and I am eternally grateful "to the only wise God our Savior." To Him be "glory and majesty, dominion and power, both now and ever" (Jude 1:25, KJV). Amen.

In your quest to birth your visions or dreams, you may face a lot of obstacles. Things may get worse before getting better. Don't give up. This lesson was reinforced to me after an experience I had with a misplaced flash drive.

One day my husband used my laptop, disconnected my flash drive from the laptop, but he returned the laptop with no flash drive. As I settled in the next morning to start working, my flash drive was nowhere to be found. I texted my hubby who had left the house if he remembered where he kept my flash drive, but he didn't.

I desperately needed some information on that flash drive. But, I had this bad habit of leaving it plugged into my laptop rather than disconnecting it when no longer in use.

So, I began the search. I looked everywhere I could possibly think of multiple times, but after two and a half hours, I was discouraged. I almost gave up the search for my flash drive.

Thankfully, my husband returned home around that time, and he began another search for the flash drive. He searched places that I had already searched and places that I didn't think of searching.

As he was searching, I told him to stop wasting his time because I didn't think we could successfully locate the flash drive. I told him that I probably had some of the same information in my email and that I would rebuild from there, and that he should no longer bother looking for the flash drive as it was time-consuming and frustrating. Of course, my hubby decided to persevere and I decided to give it one more go, and thankfully, he found the flash drive! In that moment, I realized that I had almost given up at the brink of my breakthrough. I would like to encourage you to hang in there! Your next try may end up being your best try. You can take all that you have learned in your past attempts and failures and give it another go.

"Let us not become weary in doing good, for at the proper time we will reap a harvest if we do not give up." — *Galatians 6:9 (NIV)*

The proper time is closer than you think. Be encouraged!

GET IN POSITION; YOUR BABY IS ON ITS WAY!

When a woman is in delivery mode and having contractions, she knows that her bundle of joy, that she has waited nine months for, is finally arriving in a matter of hours. At this point, she is not worried about her phone, her hair, or other trivial things. She is a woman on a mission-focused on getting that baby out. First, the contractions are far apart, and her cervix is not dilating. Even if she goes to the hospital, she may be sent back home. However, when those contractions are active and close to one another and she is 10 cm dilated, it's time to push-though she may be in pain.

You may be right on the edge of your breakthrough, but you are in so much pain and agony. It is not the time to give up; you have a baby that is getting ready to come out, and we can already see the head! Your visions, your dreams, your business, and your calling are almost here. You can't hire a surrogate to birth your destiny. By God's grace, you won't have a stillbirth or any damaging complications with your destiny. Take deep breaths, and when the pain of contraction hits you, push through it. You need to be more focused than ever, have a tunnel vision of what you want to accomplish and pusshh. Try again, try harder, pray like you have never prayed before, and take some time to fast if you must. Pusshhh! Do not be afraid. Just push!

> *"For the Spirit God gave us does not make us timid, but gives us power, love and self-discipline."* — *2 Timothy 1:7 (NIV)*
>
> *"Have I not commanded you? Be strong and courageous. Do not be afraid; do not be discouraged, for the LORD your God will be with you wherever you go."* — *Joshua 1:9 (NIV)*

You are facing many uncertainties, you don't know if you can handle taking care of the baby (your vision, dreams, ideas, etc.), and you wonder if you will fail. But it doesn't matter. Just pusshhh. God has got your back. He has been preparing you for nine months or nine years. It doesn't matter what anyone says about you or how anyone feels about you, you have what it takes to birth that baby. If God says you are ready, then you are ready.

This "baby" is the reason why "they" tried to silence you. This "baby" is the reason why "they" rejected you. This "baby" is the reason why you have been going through all those challenges, struggles, and pain. Your baby is going to bruise the head of the serpent. Your baby is going to destroy the works of the devil. Your baby is going to bring glory to God, so take another deep breath and pusshhh! Congratulations!

Your baby is here in the name of Jesus!

Chapter 7

SERVE GOD

○

Something else that my family and I are committed to doing is serving the Lord. Serving God comes in different forms.

> *"Whatever you do, work heartily, as for the Lord and not for men, knowing that from the Lord you will receive the inheritance as your reward. You are serving the Lord Christ." — Colossians 3:23–24 (ESV)*

Based on the above Scripture, you can serve God wherever you are in whatever you do with all your heart. Whatever you find your hands doing, do it as unto the Lord.

> *"Whoever is kind to the poor lends to the LORD, and he will reward them for what they have done." — Proverbs 19:17 (NIV)*

God is also delighted when we help people who are genuinely in need. I pray that God gives us the wisdom to know when to act and how to help those in need around us.

"The LORD watches over the foreigner and sustains the fatherless and the widow, but he frustrates the ways of the wicked." — Psalm 146:9 (NIV)

We can also help foreigners around us because in many cases, they are new to the area and are starting their lives all over again. Also, children who have only one parent or no parents need our support. It truly takes a village to raise them. Widows or widowers may also need our help. They may have recently lost a spouse who was the breadwinner, may be grieving and may not even have any family members who can help. God feels the pain of people who are brokenhearted, and we are encouraged to help them if we can.

VOLUNTEER AT YOUR LOCAL CHURCH

We can also serve God in our local Bible-believing church. Many churches have areas of need or opportunities for volunteers to serve, including church cleaning, children's ministry, choir, ushers, prayer team, etc.

The very first church I volunteered in, I was in the youth ministry and taught Sunday school, and I also helped clean up after major events in the church.

When I started serving God, I got into a space of accountability. The people of God lovingly held a mirror up to my face, and for the first time in my life, I saw myself for who I really was. And for the first time, I received the courage to begin the work on myself.

Until this point in my life, I always ran away from working on myself. Working on yourself is uncomfortable and it can be painful, but it is necessary to birth your visions and dreams.

When that mirror is held up to you and you see yourself, it may first trigger the victim mentality. You think you are being attacked by the person holding up the mirror, and if you are like I was, you begin to attack the messenger; the person holding up the mirror. I have been on both ends; the person holding up the mirror and the person looking in the mirror. Regardless of which part you play, it's not easy. You must focus on the result; there is beauty at the end of your story.

LESSONS LEARNED FROM MENTORS

I learned obedience and self-control. It is important for us to practice obedience with the God-given authority around us and get used to it. Otherwise, it would be difficult to obey God and His Word.

We should obey Godly authority, even if they are not necessarily the nicest, provided they are God-sent and telling you the right thing. What we need to understand about mentors is that they are sent to give life and resuscitate parts of you that are dead. Focus on the message, not the messenger, as mentors are not angels but flesh and blood and may deliver the message imperfectly. And if you focus on the messenger, you may get distracted.

While serving God, I learned how to act around people, how to communicate with people, and how to control myself when upset. This is important because some of us are like a car without brakes. We need to be able to get a grip on our emotions before it wrecks us. I learned all these from people who corrected me; being open and willing to accept their correction, and from being around people who were stronger in my areas of weakness and emulating them. I put myself in a position where my wrongs could be exposed and corrected in love and with time. It was an uncomfortable position, but one that yielded growth and maturity.

HOW TO DEAL WITH CHURCH HURT

While serving God, I have had a lot of heartache, and I have seen sides of people that have caused me pain. I have also learned how to handle such situations.

When someone hurts your feelings in church, you need to have the right perspective. First, church is supposed to be for people who are hurting and broken to come as they are to the foot of the cross for healing. It is to be expected that hurting people may hurt you, and broken people may break your heart. So, even at church, you need to ask the Lord to give you your friends and for wisdom to navigate different personalities. Secondly, you should recognize that as perfect as you may think you are, you may have offended people at one point or another, and someone at some point must have forgiven you. So, you also should learn to forgive.

> *"Make allowance for each other's faults, and forgive anyone who offends you. Remember, the Lord forgave you, so you must forgive others." — Colossians 3:13 (NLT)*

NO STRIFE

Also, you should not leave a church only because your feelings got hurt. Our feelings get hurt at work, among family members, and in other spheres of life, and we don't immediately leave those groups. We should seek the Lord for direction on whatever He wants us to do. If God wants you to stay, then stay, learn, and grow. If God says it is time for you to leave, then leave. Communicate God's direction with the appropriate church leader and work with them as you peacefully exit the church. Lastly, do not cause strife or collaborate with people who are causing strife.

"A dishonest man spreads strife, and a whisperer separates close friends." — Proverbs 16:28 (ESV)

"So then let us pursue what makes for peace and for mutual upbuilding." — Romans 14:19 (ESV)

"Behold, all who are incensed against you shall be put to shame and confounded; those who strive against you shall be as nothing and shall perish." — Isaiah 41:11 (ESV)

If people whisper all sorts of negative information to you about the church you attend or people in the church, be very careful not to join with them in such chatter. If there is a genuine issue, the issue can be discussed with the church leadership. However, if you join a conspiracy of whisperers to spread strife in and about a church, Isaiah 41:11 speaks of the consequences. It is better for you to say nothing and leave quietly than engage in strife that isn't God-sanctioned. Please don't allow people to pull you into their mess.

CONCLUSION

---○---

Aren't you glad that you don't look like what you have been through? I know that life sometimes hits you hard and you are left to put the broken pieces of your life back together, but with God on your side, you can be made whole! You may look at other people's lives on Instagram and it may seem like everyone has it together except for you, but remember that things are not always what they seem like. You may be a single mom, but you can still accomplish your goals in life. You may be divorced, but you can still be all that God has called you to be. You may feel like people look down on you, but you don't have to let that stop you from being your best. You may feel unloved by people, but you can receive the unfailing and immeasurable love of your heavenly father. You may be in pain over a problem, but you can overcome life's challenges. You may feel like people don't like you, but don't stay focused on that because there are a host of others who do like you. You may have given up on your dreams, but I want you to know that your best is yet to come! You may feel like you don't have what it takes to succeed in life, but I want you to know that as long as you have breath, you can birth your visions and dreams.

www.ingramcontent.com/pod-product-compliance
Lightning Source LLC
Chambersburg PA
CBHW071933020426
42331CB00010B/2852